MALE'IN IT

By

Carl Nixon

ISBN: 1-4033-1575-2 (E-book)
ISBN: 1-4033-1576-0 (Paperback)
ISBN: 1-4107-2338-0 (Dust Jacket)

This book is printed on acid free paper.

1stBooks – rev 03/17/03

Table of contents

Finding the right companion

When I'm weak there's no cure in the world like female companionship, whether you're my lover or just a female friend, you talking and listening to me In my time of need can put things In my heart as a man that will carry with me qualities strapped in me to give to practically any woman I meet.

The females that don't mind giving me time and listening to what I got to say with no strings attached are truly gods blessings that keep me wanting and understanding woman, and not to just sex them up and move on, because through them I punch on knowing there's still truly great women to meet, to learn, and to come to love.

Truly great men seem to be lost in the freight and no doubt passed up by the women of true value and love it seems because so many immature females push and shove to get to the front of our attention then have the nerve to not bring no substance at all to a relationship, besides a nice body and stuck up ways, as a result you have a lot of failing couples and a lot of real women who's willing to treat a man all the way right suffering and missing out on real men.

…But I guess I'll keep searching.

Carl Nixon

Females and periods

Females forgive me If I don't catch the hint when you're on your period, perhaps If you we're a bit more comfortable in talking about your periods with me I might understand you a little better when your behavior patterns change. Around that time of the month you make me want to run In a hole and hide until its over but I'm not a female so I can't possibly totally understand what you go through.

I want to apologize for not only myself but for all men like me who you can drop a bucket of blood on a week straight of your period and we still won't catch the hint and be compassionate when we should be.

I really do understand your period conditions are a part of your nature and that's a fact I have no problem living with, just remind me from time to time.

Carl Nixon

Baby Daddy's

Its unlikely that everyone will get married but it is likely that most will have children, then the strong likely hood that many will part.

The biological father if he's any type of man at all should be a part of his children's lives because when children become adults they remember things and who played major roles.

I assume a lot of females don't let the biological father be a real part of their child or children's lives because of cheating on his part, not really knowing or succeeding at what he want in life, and or aren't simply there in the ways a real father should be.

For all those "out to do nothing dads" all of them need to wake up handle there responsibilities and be fathers, and females should lighten up more on fathers who really want to be there and be a part.

…Because you know who suffer.

Carl Nixon

Physical punishment on children

Physical beating of a child only seem to be applied when parents let the initial proper disciplining slip by.

If a parent or the parents instill aggressively in children verbal and hand slap traits the first time and every time thereafter when a child acts badly I almost guarantee they will respect and obey their elders far past adulthood.

The problem might be that many parents are too soft when it come to raising children, they look at them as being so loveable and let them get away with murder until its to late.

People say that other races spoil and don't discipline their children properly, and others say that most African Americans beat their children into submissions, but I say its the weak minded parents that don't have their own acts together and lash out physically on children no matter what race you are.

I've seen just about every race there is raise their children different ways, some through physical spankings and some through the mental off hands approach.

Whatever the case I believe different children need different doses of discipline to achieve the right upbringing, and it's up to each individual parent to know their children and what disciplinary actions they need.

Carl Nixon

Mental Abuse

This is no doubt the most stressing part of a relationship to me, females don't know how much this affects me, my well being, and how in turn I treat you.

As a man I'm hurt by a woman the only way I can be, in the head, and the men that lash out physically do so a lot of times because they've had it to the ceiling with mental abuse and haven't the patience to deal with problems on a rational level.

It would do a female a world of good to treat me as you would your friend or friends" and if that's with respect, kindness when speaking to them, always being enjoyable without a thought around them, and sharing endlessly I don't see where we could ever go wrong.

I never can understand why females don't take their girlfriend' approach anyway when dealing with their men" things would work out a lot better.

Carl Nixon

Raising a girl

Raising a boy to me come so natural I do it without much effort at all, a girl however complicates me because I don't truly know everything needed or need to be said to give her the greatest chances of becoming a real woman, I can only act off instincts and speculation.

Same gender raising can be vital to a child's upbringing, and if I we're a single parent dad raising a girl I would definitely have a female role model or girlfriend around to assist me in the ways of raising her that only a female knows, any other way or without a female presence in place could be wrong and damaging.

Carl Nixon

Television' and media

Freedom of speech my backside! every adult and network controller to me has an obligation to our children to show them righteous and moral programming, set positive examples, and not to show sex, violence, and drug contents where they know it can and will be made available young children's way, but I guess it's too late to ask for that.

Call me old fashion but I'd rather see my child or children raised by more sources than myself, because I know while I can direct their path ultimately society will probably play a major role in tipping their scales.

Most children listen to their parents as I did but I also knew in my little heart I was going to listen to television and bad influences to help raise me as well.

To raise children the full and proper way in today's societies I don't know the solution but people should be more censoring, because it does affect a great many kids and what they become.

Children are so innocent, and exposing the weakest to acts they can't quite handle yet could have major consequences, ...and often do.

Carl Nixon

Needing to bond with the guys

Like it or not I need to bond with the guys, whether it's just hanging out or them coming by once in a while.

It's best for our relationship when you're more accepting of my male companions because that tell me you trust me, and it's not all about you, and in all essence that's the only life outside of one another we really have, our associates, loved ones, and friends.

Many females tend to worry about their boyfriend's cheating on them when hanging out with the guys, well I can tell you now, there's no man in the world that can make me fool around on you if I really love you and want to be with you, if I fool around on you its because of something you can't or refuse to give me.

...If you're the one, and you know it, you need not worry about anything.

Carl Nixon

Gangs drugs and street violence

Being from the east and mid west part of the country I don't see or hear about as many gangs as out west, however drug selling and street violence happens everywhere. I don't agree with drug selling killing and violence because ultimately it ends in fear and or death in a breeding society where young children are followers.

I would brace those young men and boys who really don't know what they're getting into because these dangers isn't no joke.

I figure those caught up in the drug and violence world probably have no positive role models to steer and keep them on the right path to get jobs and make honest livings, on the flip side I've always been a realist and I don't see it ever being or have ever been enough jobs for every man, woman, and teenage girl and boy who qualifies to work when there's only so many jobs to go around at once... But neither is violence the key.

Carl Nixon

Me and the law

What's up with cops and the law? I can't front, I'm totally down with our laws of the land, and I certainly haven't had the best relations with them, but we need cops and the law to keep me, you, and our children safe, and to me that far outweigh any questioned speeding ticket or harassments I may have.

I don't believe there'd be a civilized neighborhood around if the hands of the law weren't there to intervene and protect us every time a situation got out of hand and lives were harmed.

I just hope and pray that god remain with me, my loved ones, and friends, to keep us on the right side of the law and keep us safe and honest to always do the right thing.

...I recognize there are bad officers and hands of the law like anything else, so I salute those who are honest, and uphold true godly values to protect us.

Always shouts! to you because I never feel enough attention is credited to the freedom you provide.

Carl Nixon

Why sports

If you have a man like me you have sports in your life, understanding me can probably be seen from sports and being physical. Sports does for me what perhaps decorating a home does for you.

Sports is endurance, and takes me from the tired cycles of life to a new charged thinker and doer.

Many women don't know the connection to being physically fit and the performances of everyday life for me, but I perform well in bed or otherwise because I work out doing physical activities or have a physically charge mind.

My everyday hinges on being fit mentally and or physically, and quite simply, being involved in sports some kind of way keeps my mind and body strong enough for you.

Carl Nixon

Other women in waiting

With me' other women in waiting use to be a natural instinct, maybe it was the worry and wonder that I was never certain of my future with one woman.

In most cases I need to be shown how much I'm loved and appreciated, something a lot of females don't provide.

If a female want to delete all possibilities of me even wanting to give my time to someone else she should make absolutely sure I'm happy with her, not to say she must be at my becking call, but perhaps go that extra mile in acknowledging and adhering to the things that really make me happy and content, and try to give them to me.

It would be nice to know that you know and care enough to satisfy my needs without me giving you play by play accounts all the time, this to me is important and keeps my mind from the thoughts of other women being able to fulfill something in me you can't or won't.

Carl Nixon

Blind dates and dating

I just want to know one thing! who judges females? who hands them their grades during and after dates? who rejects them? guess who! nobody!

Maybe you have or haven't heard of the blind dating show that comes on television, but why does it always seem one sided where the men are sweating bullets to make great first impressions while the females sit back and relish the opportunities to see us put our foot in our mouths so they can say ok! you don't deserve me!

If a man haven't much to say on a date or a blind date he's a loser, but if a female haven't much to say she just has an upset stomach, or something like that.

Point is a lot of females don't give men fair shots when it come to their self patience to get to know us, but absolutely demand it when it come to getting to know them, and no matter how foolish females may look their excuses are always justified.

Blind dating or dating for me sucks today because females put to much pressure on a man to be perfect.

Carl Nixon

Sex first then I'll commit, Maybe

Females make a lot of commitment before sex but yet It would be you later that will say I can't please you if I don't perform well.

Lets keep it real, if you go out with me' enjoy my company, we laugh and have good times together then you want to finally go all the way with me and I'm whack, that may start a roving eye and perhaps cheating on your part, and you having the nerve to believe you're doing the right thing because I can't please you like you feel a man should.

This type of thing could only happen if you want to get to know me first then fall head over hills in love with me as a person but haven't yet tasted my sexual waters to see if I'll be all that you'll ever need, and in all honesty that wouldn't be fair to either of us to commit to a relationship where we don't know whether our body chemistry even mix.

…I say test my water first…but with protection, that is, if you intend to get involved with a man intimately before marriage.

Carl Nixon

Female body builders

I have to give credit to female bodybuilders for achieving what most men don't have, top quality physiques.

I have to admire female bodybuilders for beating the challenges of being fit, but when it come to dating and mating with them their probably just not for me, even if I was a top notch body builder myself.

While a female bodybuilder and myself might get along exceptionally well on a mind and friendship basis, when it come to intimate relations I don't think I could mesh.

Some female bodybuilders feel that the average man is intimidated by them and scared to date them, I say that simply their not feminine enough for me, because I don't take pleasure in being intimate with a body sculptured like a man.

...Call me crazy, but how can I get a chemical reaction for a body that's more masculine than mine.

Carl Nixon

Want to marry me, don't press

If you want this hand in marriage you probably should wait until I ask you, if you press and it go through you may not receive all you need from me, because quite frankly I wasn't really ready to get married in the first place, at least not at that time to you.

The reasons I marry you could be endless, I could need you, I could be alone and afraid, and I could be simply using you.

When I'm truly ready to get married you will know it because I'll do all the things written to try and make you happy.

If a woman want the real from me in a marriage its best if she wait until I ask for her hand in marriage.

A pressured marriage when I'm not ready brings from me nothing but arguments, infidelity, and sometimes hate.

Carl Nixon

Good looks vs. Bad

If you have good looks naturally you get first dibs on me, and if you look bad you probably won't have no dibs at all, but not really because if you have a nice personality, a sense of humor, can be a great lover, and strong willed and healthy, in my eyes you can fulfill the shoes of beauty my foolish eyes and body feel it need. Its really sad that often we're judged on our outward appearance because we really miss out on someone special.

I don't really discriminate against looks, but there are lots of people who do, so I say to those that's put down for your looks to keep your head's up, and invite people in and around your life that treat you right, there's always someone that can be just as accommodating and mending for your aching heart.

...Remember, you're the first and most important person in your life and looking after your own happiness and confidence should be first, don't settle for someone who think their better than you and will treat you less than what you deserve, because the way I see it everyone is equal...

Carl Nixon

I like you don't push it

If you want to get time from me don't push me, I'll only give you what I'm feeling you're worth, and a big part of that is how you come off to me. If and until I really decide its you I indeed want to be with, come to know and love, it seems only fair that you allow me that time to decide for myself,don't push me to make decisions you or I may regret.

It seem to me it's logical to date other people because it's the only sure way of finding your mate, if you find one at all because far to many relationships exist and are sewn on couples just liking one another with no real growth or potential, then end up only hating one another and being together in unfulfilled relationships. If I just like you let it be at that, if we're true soul mates we will come together on our own, lets not get it twisted in humble beginnings, because to me' love runs deeper than just good times, sex, and laughs.

Carl Nixon

I want children but not with you

If you want to bear my child or children I first need to ask myself am I the man for you, are you the woman for me, will our child or children be best suited with us as parents, and will I really want to be there and be a part of your lives.

If you don't have righteous values, no mental smarts, weak minded, don't possess the qualities I feel a mother should, and have your game face on for life to raise kids, chances are you're not the one.

I want a lady and a woman rolled into one to become the bearer of my children, because I know with this come many blessings, love, and shared right upraising for mine.

If I don't see in you intention to be a homemaker, and or have true capability to build a family, chances are you bet not dream of having children with me and me liking it.

Children deserve parents who don't have issues at hand that will affect them in some way or fashion, and who can family them in the proper way, because to many females have children out of wedlock without the proper ways or means of raising them.

37

Carl Nixon

Save your male compliments

It never cease to amaze me how my opposite sex compliment and sometimes over compliment other men in my presence as if I'm suppose to like it.

From my stand point its one of my first priorities upon meeting or being around a female, to not salivate over or compliment other females in her presence, yet females seem to love to slap the male compliments on thick around me totally lost at how I might feel.

Of course you love men and are attracted to them but I'm not, and I find it rather uncomforting and rather disrespectful for females to speak out of other men as though I'm no where in sight.

No! It's not an ego thing, I just believe if something's uncomfortable for me or not in common with the way I think it should be respected, and shouldn't be talked about or discussed with or around me, because females don't like it when men hawk and praise other females around them.

...Save your male complimenting for your girlfriends... I won't mind at all.

Carl Nixon

Ego heads

Females of this caliber take the cake, often it appear that their so into themselves and their own world that they can't decipher a line from the truth when being approached, from the start their often hotheaded, obnoxious, and rude, with respect only for what they feel is candy to their eyes.

For the females who'll turn their nose up at me before I can point my toes to walk your way tells me you're selfish and not fair, because I just refuse to believe every man you're being approached by don't meet your standard's, you just won't look far enough into men to see different qualities.

Females with a little going on for themselves have grown up being catered to and handed things on a platter probably so often they don't know or haven't taken the time to know a quality person when they see or meet one, not to mention the social skills they lack in just general conversations.

I imagine more down to earth nice mannered females have more fun out of life and not find themselves letting life pass them by because their not captivated in their own beauty, and so stuck up they can't come down, but hey! that's cool with me, with so many lovelies in the world to choose from with winner attitudes and personalities to die for who needs them.

Carl Nixon

Gold diggers

I hate gold diggers because their insensitive and in' compassionate. How can any female take a man for whatever she can get from him without thinking how that might affect him or his financial status.

Men give freely many times to females because we love and adore you, and for that I don't feel our generosity should be taken advantage of.

Females that will get involved with a man with preplanned plans to get what they can from him then skip not caring what type of financial limbo they leave him in are the females to me that don't deserve happiness until they repent.

Gold diggers in my opinion are in a class by themselves and will step on and over anybody to get where their going.

…Then again we have a lot of suckers! out here who shower them, so I guess I'll let them worry about it.

Carl Nixon

Plus size women

Plus size women are truly some of the nicest godly treating caring people I ever want to meet, if its because their overweight, feel self conscious, and tend to feel they should treat people a little kinder to be accepted they shouldn't, because more men then you know will date and even marry and establish relationship's with plus women because besides their mental strengths their soft lovein equally equates as well.

Smaller built females seem to mess over men all the time, probably figuring they can get practically any man they want, all the while losing sight of the equality they really need to be bringing to relationships.

Of course slimmer and medium built females have good qualities to, but because their often pursued they don't always bring the right attitudes.

I've seen countless smaller females go unhappy in life because they put themselves on such high planks they become out of reach for anyone down to earth and genuine, therefore missing all the action with quality men that submit to plus females who keep it real and make it their business and prioritiy to be family women'.

Carl Nixon

You're weak when it come to sex

As strong as females profess to be you are truly the weakest being's in the world when men" get past the doors and actually get to the good part.

Every female I've ever heard about or been with in a sexual manner didn't seem to take much at all to entice into sex acts, and slam the condom against the wall before ever using it if I choose to do so.

With all the senseless sex and diseases going around nowadays you never know where your next trap door is, and females got it bad when it come to male sexual persuasion.

If you're a female that don't like using condoms and protection you need to pray and abstain, or your partner and you go in to be tested together for diseases before you make a pack, life's to short, men talk to fast, and you are easily bowled over by maleness.

Don't let a smooth talking, joke maker laugh you out your panties without protecting yourself, or getting you involved in sexual acts you may regret later.

…Just a reminder to be strong.

Carl Nixon

Me and strippers

When I go to a strip club It probably wouldn't be out of order to say I might have hopes of getting fondled and or possibly laid by a female stripper. Some men say they go to a strip club to get charged up to go home and make love to their women, this may be true for some but certainly not all.

Personally if I'm visiting strip clubs chances are I'm not totally being fulfilled at home, or my woman simply isn't enough to please me. Liken to it I believe that any female that visit male strip clubs have sexual issues at home, though I do believe females are a little better at not getting involved with the dancers they go to see.

Some strippers make a bad name for the rest of the dancers by selling themselves for profit, then there are others that strip simply as a means of moving ahead, these are the ones I seem to respect most.

Dancers that strip simply for the money and prostitute themselves are the ones I tend to respect least because they seem to always be the ones that talk about how tricks pay them and buy them things.

I just feel if you're going to strip, do it with class and a means to make a better life for yourself instead of being absorbed in it just for the sex, money, and praise.

49

Carl Nixon

Offer me a drink and conversation

If more females would trade places, approach me at different functions, and offer to buy me a drink and perhaps ask me for a dance and maybe a little conversation this would be a much better place to live for me.

You think you have power now, if you knew the power respect and attention you'd get from me by being a little more assertive and coming on to me you wouldn't believe it.

If you're going to take hours getting ready and smelling good to come out and impress me, you should at least sometimes play it all the way up, approach me and offer me a drink and a dance, it would be so much easier for me to relax and be myself instead of feeling compelled to talk over loud music where I only end up sounding like a plum fool anyway.

If you would drop everything once in a while and put forth effort to approach and get to know me we might get along much better once and if we ever become any kind of companions at all.

Me approaching you over loud music and voices in a loud club nine out of ten times will not be on point with you because you can't hear what the heck I'm trying to say to you, instead my best conversations are stumped before they get started, and we all know how totally unfair, misleading, and down right straight forward doggish females can be if I roll up on you half stepping!

...I think it's only fair.

51

Carl Nixon

Most men are jerks, Try blaming you

Because of role playing, different approaches, and silly games ran by all' the faces have changed in my opinion in connecting.

Females have set the standard so high in the men they look for I don't know what to say upon meeting or talking to you, and if my first line of conversation doesn't hit your buttons you think I'm a jerk.

I blame females, because most of the time it is you who shoot me down because I can't read your mind right away and know what it is you want from me.

Would you really blame and judge me on the stupid blocks I stumble over just to get to know you? Are you really out to seek and conquer the opposite sex to treat with love and respect? Or are you so set in your own selfish ways to prejudge that you can't think straight?

Most men that appear to be jerks that really aren't I believe are mostly perceived by stereotypical females who don't look past their own selfishness, their first meetings, don't instantly see the qualities they look for in men, and or are simply not interested and file us away under jerks.

...You that judge so quickly are truly the self centered jerks.

...I don't know where this leave men and our approach to females if we don't want to be pegged total idiots over fumbled conversations, and one thing always seem sure, the same words that offend one might not offend another, and lovely conversation from some could be harassing to others.

...I guess the real bottom line is...you're only a jerk in the eyes of the beholders.

Cheating

I always believed people remain faithful because they know how to position themselves to stay out of temptations way.How many people can really be faithful, I guess that might depend on your situation at home, what's before you, and where you are.

If my sex life is suffering and I find myself in a tempted setting with a female I'm attracted to I could get weak and give in if she present sexual advances, that's why for me it's important to be able to stay away from any circumstances I can't control, and if I truly love the woman I'm with I'll avoid these situations at all cost.

Sometimes supposedly devoted couples cheat because they allow themselves to merge into situations they shouldn't be near and know they don't have the self controlling nature to maintain abstinence.

For me to desire other females would not be the crime, the crime would be for being around other females that I know I'm attracted to, then allowing myself to allow the thought then the execution of getting involved while already in a relationship.

...My best shot in all honesty to stay loyal would probably be to stay out of compromising situations.

Carl Nixon

Hollow queen

If a female is going to act queen in some ways than sour in others how can I respect you and pronounce you queen of all I'll ever need. I believe the goal of practically every man and every woman is to find love, peace, wealth, and happiness, and every man deserve to be treated like king and every woman queen, and when I'm not getting that treatment to me that say I'm not important enough for you, in turn I'll hold out on my true feelings and treat you as a hollow queen until a woman that will truly love and respect me the way I need it come along, of course that may never happen and you'll forever just be a replacement for the woman I wish I had.

If you really want to be my queen and not just fill a void treat me right, this would be a great way of truly making me consider you to be queen of my life.

Carl Nixon

Marriage before thirty

I would like to say thirty five but for argument sake I'll just say I believe the age of thirty should be the age of people when truly considering getting married.

When you're in your teens and twenties how can you possibly know and be ready for something as serious as marriage when you don't even fully know who you are.

Because you think you're in love, have great sex, share fun bliss and laughs together, and or because you've had and or having a child or children you think you're ready for marriage.

To truly make a marriage work it will take hard sacrifice that many couples aren't willing to give until their at least in their thirties.

The paperwork can wait what's important is to access and evaluate your own life to see if you're really ready to take such a major step on holy ground, and quite frankly I believe when you're a teenager and in your twenties you have so much to live for you can't possibly be ready for such a commitment, not to mention whether you even have the strength and loyalty in you.

...If you like to party, enjoy open sex, easily influenced, and don't have moral faith, these are just a few things you might want to look at before taking the marriage step...

...Just my opinion.

Of course, there are teen' and twenty something' relationships that last, just none I've ever heard of.

Street prostitution and sluts

Street prostitution and sluts are without question at the front wheel of sexual health breakdowns.

For whatever reason's many men will go to the streets of prostitution or lay up with sluts to receive the sexual pleasures they can get from their own wives or girlfriends.

Street hookers perform any and every sexual pleasure all day long for cheap prices, and the diseases they leave men with certainly isn't worth it.

Almost all sexually transmitted diseases in my opinion starts in the streets from average men who have sexual intercourse with prostitutes and or sluts, then take the diseases back home to their wives or girlfriends.

I can't imagine why a man would pay for sexual favors and or sleep with trampy females that's been around when it's so many well kept females in the world to pursue and choose from.

It's sad that people claim someone well enough to sleep with measured by the time they've known them rather than getting their medical sexual histories, because from this behavior many people have and will continue to be affected.

Carl Nixon

Three way sex, not with my love

I say this for one reason only, the woman I come to love and want to spend my life with I want to be just that, a straight woman.

A lot of women tend to believe that every man fantasy is two women at once, don't just assume I want to see you get it on with another woman because my real bottom line is a one on one with a woman I can love and trust and that don't want anyone else but me, furthermore I don't believe in encouraging and turning females out.

If a man want to experience or live a three way lifestyle he should do it with bisexual or lesbian females who'll have him, because going as far as trying to change or sway a straight female in this manner to me is one of the worst ungodly sins to commit.

…Don't get it twisted, two females at once I'm not against, but its not something I have to have, and if I engage at all it would be with two females I don't love.

Carl Nixon

Interracial relationships

Interracial dating isn't a big deal to me anymore but if you're a person who cares about what others think of you perhaps you should reconsider your intimate relations outside your race, but as long as two people really like and can come to love one another it shouldn't be anyone else's business.

From my perspective females play so hard to get nowadays I tend to settle for whatever female is willing to give me quality time and treat me like a man, and if she's of another creed and she and I are blessed to come each other's way so be it.

Any female that's willing to acknowledge old tradition and giving and doing the things she know I need to be comfortable and successful is the female that I need in my life, and personally I don't discriminate.

I find that many interracial relationships are born out of sheer circumstance, association, and being in the same inner circles anyway, so how can anyone really blame or judge anyone else for who they meet and become an item with.

If I'm lucky enough to find someone that makes me happy and that really care for me I'm going for it because there's no guarantee or law that says I'll find success and happiness in all fairness at all with anyone.

Carl Nixon

All men are dogs, Don't be foolish

If you think that all men are dogs and you really believe it you have a serious problem" or either you know how and where to look for the good men and choose not to. The same females that call all men dogs I think are often the same females that don't want to look where righteous and honest men can be found instead prancing around in the areas where major dogs breed.

Men might be out of control and female greedy at times, but that's due to your flaunty wear and never ending enticements.

Most of the time the females that end up with dog men know exactly what their getting in their men" and decide to go ahead with them anyway in hopes of changing them.

Are these also the type of female's that go out their way to make me lose my mind and composure over how unbearably attractive and wanting they are then accuse me of being a dog.

I know there's major dogs out here, but please don't log us all in until you've gotten to know us individually, because men are no more dogs then you are...if you mean...watchdogs.

Carl Nixon

Pushing stripper fantasies on straight women

Why would any man try to encourage his girlfriend or wife to visit and receive lap dances from females at female strip clubs" when clearly their not interested and will tell you so. I like to call these boys that will end up losing their partners because real men know this is something you simply don't do.

Men do things to uplift a female and keep her pure in all her ways, and never take advantage of her weaknesses for his self gain and distort and send her into an immoral lifestyle against her will.

Sexual fantasies should be mutual to be of any significance, but a lot of them are pushed on weaker females that don't know how to say no to what they really don't want and or to be involved in, choosing rather to please the men they're with.

...I guess this boil down to what an individual will stand for.

Carl Nixon

During sex I better be the bomb

Females without a doubt will probably agree that not only the first sex encounter but practically everyone thereafter a man better perform well with you because if not he might not get another chance to prove himself superman.

Of course its not the same when it come to pleasing me, all you have to do is be there and you just about deserve an A.

I don't know where it came from or how it got started that men have to be the ultimate bed pleasers, then I don't suppose it matter, this one rule that will never change.

Carl Nixon

Me and breast

Females often complain that all men see is their breast, frankly speaking I'm a leg, thigh, and butt man first, you can have breast for days, without nice legs and a nice backside you might be passed up without second thought, as a matter of fact if your waist down is tight and you have a head on your shoulders you won't need much breasts at all to attract a guy like me, I might say the waist below attributes" in a female get my chemicals running.

Of course I find breast attractive but if you have personality, style, and those other physical parts I spoke about that far out weigh any lack you may have physically. Big breasted females don't be angered at me if I'm attractive to your breast, by nature they were designed for me to look at, and if you expose them in any way I may get a glimpse I'm going to look...

I suppose if men of all cuts, colors, and sizes graced the earth half nude and exploited and exposed themselves daily like females do the female agenda probably couldn't and wouldn't control their sexual energies either... So stop tripp'in!

...And yes! I do understand a lot of men cross the line all the time and make the rest of us appear one track minded, but don't assume all.

Carl Nixon

Sexual harassment

I still don't understand this law.

I figure I feel this way because I overheard females planning to bring sexual harassment suits against guys for return flirting, you know! when females think their interested so they do things to egg men on, then we do things to turn you off completely all of a sudden you realize you're no longer interested and us poor guys can't or don't catch the hints to back off all of a sudden we're sliding on a lawsuit.

Any woman filing a sexual harassment lawsuit should first before filing summons the harasser, work supervisors, their superiors, sit down together issue written warnings to the admitted harasser, then the victim and harasser establish good faith handshakes of apology, this to me only seem fair because its of my uncontrollable nature to sometimes lose control and cross the line a little when it come to you.

I just never believed in my heart that uncontrolled attraction on the part of boys and men' in perhaps wrong family up bringing warrants them losing their jobs, futures, and possibly families and friends while the harassed females walk off with fat paychecks and a little bumped up from male compliments and advances.

Carl Nixon

Despising rapist

Its not fair that men can't stop females from teasing our loins and giving us all kind of fits just to get next to you, but its definitely not fair that some men can't control their hormones and self control then go out and rape.

I suppose I could say to all the females that don't want to be raped to stay covered up and stay at home, but for the rest of us non rapist of the world that would be like watching television without a picture, life would be no fun.

There's no excuse in the world for rape and any fool that does need to be shot between the eyes and hung upside down to drain dry.

Perhaps females should upon any such fools caught, tie pool balls in their mouths, tie their prick's to door knobs, and ram the hell out of them! with fat bats.

…Just be careful.

Carl Nixon

Gays in the scouts and militaries

Being a man my first thought is absolutely not! my last thought is not! but I'm not god so I don't judge, but why would you confuse young children who don't even know who they are yet.

The moral issue is what do you want to offer the children, what are they acceptable to, and are they weak minded about they're own sexuality and were leaning toward being straight and perhaps gay antics and homosexual persuasion by other children pushed them the other way.

I honestly can't say how I might have turned out had I been exposed to such immoral behavior at such a young age. Call me unfair or unjust but I doubt any parent who have it all upstairs would want their son or daughter around such potential behavior.

Children are by nature very sensitive and confused and a lot of times live by the control and thoughts of others whether we like it or not.

I'm a man today because I followed simple examples as a young boy...

I'm a man today because I had fatherly discipline...

I'm a man because I had uncles and male role models that constantly pointed my eye to the opposite sex...

I'm a man because I went the way of the football, the basketball, the baseball...

I'm a man because I didn't go the way of the jump rope with the lighter acting boys...

79

I'm a man because I took pleasure in stealing and breaking the heads off my sister's dolls and stealing the cakes out of their easy bake ovens...

And I'm a man because I take responsibility for my life and have become what god intended me to be a man".

Gays in the scouts and military I have a problem with because I would be quite uncomfortable getting undressed and being around someone that look and enact with me the way a female would.

...I just kind of think I have that god given right... Ya know!

Homosexuality

This is a topic I can't begin to wonder, I know people do things for money and favors,I know people do things because they can't get much else, and I know people do things out of sheer stupidity and attraction, but what I don't know is are you really born gay.

I personally care less what people do in their own bedrooms, but when you brandish homosexual behavior in front of children who will guide us into the future from where many other innocent children are sure to come, to me this is a contribution to the destruction of the world and life as we know it.

I'm not judging who you are but I will speak out to what you do if it come to self showcasing and shoving homosexual beliefs where children's eyes can see, I just seem to have a serious problem with that and a right of responsibility to see to it that children know this behavior is wrong, not biological, and certainly not biblical, and there's no way in the world this could possibly be moral and the right thing to do.

I have sympathy for those caught up in the life style that really don't want to be, and since its now a part of our societies and gay couples will' be together I do believe laws and rights should be put in place to protect and benefit them as well.

Carl Nixon

Religion and fakes

How can anyone say their religious and in the same breath promote wrong doings, naturally these people are fakes in my book.

People act surprised, run in fear, and pray to god not to be harmed when danger come their way, and when everything seem sunny they forget about the higher power and the righteous life they should be living.

Religion in my book doesn't distinguish to me only whether you will be saved by a mighty god, but whether you're worth even calling a person.

No one wants to take in the fact that we're perhaps living in the last days, and that everything that's seeming to happen seems to fall right in the order of which the bible says, from homosexuality and violence, to suffering and killing.

I just can't understand for the life of me why our leader's of today keep promoting and marketing the wrong messages to the world when they can clearly see it's tainting the laws of religions.

I guess there's no other explanation other than to say that the people who promote and market things to corrupt the world are the people that hold no real value to the bible and the word of god.

Carl Nixon

Straying

I'll only stray when I'm not happy and being fulfilled by you the way I need to and know you can, I don't need mystery and drama in my life as much as I need simplicity, calm, and good loving, and I'll go to the end for you no matter what level of like or love with no straying if I'm blessed with the nurturing I need from you at the present time in our relationship.

If I stray chances are I'm not happy or I'm feeling you're not giving me your all, and any female that really want to hold onto me should continue to cater to my sexual, emotional, and mental fabrics to keep my attention and to keep me from wanting any other woman.

People stray for different reasons, but in my own life' being pleased from your heart all the time is what I need to stick around.

Carl Nixon

Investing time with, you I do understand

Never believe I don't understand how important it is to spend time with you because I do, but if I'm taking care of business you need to give me that time to do so because in the streets and in society often I live by vows, and vows need to be met face to face, and that requires time needed away from you. However I do understand excessive time away from home and no quality time spent with you can be damaging to our relationship, but if I'm locked inside a situation outside of home or away from you and I'm making moves to better us as a couple cut me a little slack without always nagging so my mental focus can be straight to take care of business, because no support from you or constantly worrying about what's on your mind at home won't allow me to put my best foot forward when taking care of business and can knock me back in major ways.

Investing quality time I know is essential to holding anything together, but because I'm not always available and there when you need me doesn't mean I don't love you or that we're not together, because if you're my woman no matter where I am, I'm always yours, and you're always with me.

Carl Nixon

Your family

If I can't get the support of your family it might affect our relationship deeply, and I may hold you accountable spoken or not because the way I see it its really up to you to handle your family when it come to how they perceive me.

It shouldn't be up to me to see to it that your family see me in the right light, it wouldn't be fair to me to stumble over myself to try and be accepted by people that don't really know me like you do, so I leave it up to you to teach them' me.

Upon meeting you I'm already wondering about your family, will they like me, will they come to love and embrace me, will your brother and or brothers and father accept me because of who I am, where I come from, what I do for a living, and what I haven't quite achieved yet.

If you're really into and love me its you who should make sure your family see and understand my true values, just how serious we are as a couple, and how far you really want to go with me, because one things for sure, I'll definitely see to it that my family respect and know you.

Carl Nixon

Treat me like my mom

With any sense at all the first and only kind of love I will accept from a woman is the kind of love my mother would give, honesty, loyalty, and not last but mind space to decide right and fair what truly make me happy and support me one hundred percent, so I'm lead to believe that the only love for me or real time vested with a female would be if she have these qualities.

Ultimately in the end it'll take mother like qualities to hold me…

…The only real woman for me, would be like mom.

Carl Nixon

You make more money, I'm not trippin!

The fact is a female don't have to work at all and will probably be embraced with open arms from practically any man she meet and become involved with, but a man better have a job or some kind of income coming in to get total respect. I've seen relationships stay together when the female was the breadwinner but not many. Of course I don't agree with a man sitting around doing nothing but if I have goals and take a little more time searching and reaching my destinations females should be more supportive as men have been since the beginning of time. I don't even think I can muster myself to shun a female due to her lack of work or finance, because its not hard to see that opportunities for women today has taken major leaps over men' and sometime take men longer to succeed.

I like to believe its due to the drive and determination of females to get ahead and make better lives for themselves but the sad truth may be that jobs are being created and offered to women more.

If you make more money than me more power to you, as long as you treat me right with love and respect and not be cocky about your financial status I have no problem at all with you, because what's important to me is a grounded relationship, and a woman who will have my back and look after me in any circumstances we may have as a couple.

Carl Nixon

Older women and me

While there are females that hook up with older men you might see younger men and older women actually lasting with true devoted love relationships because on a large scale men don't seem to look to older women as a sugar source, and if they do they often end up falling in love or deeply caring .

Maybe its because older women tend to bring and give things to relationships that younger females just don't seem to grasp, not to say that younger females are wrong in their ways but rather they just don't seem to be ready for total commitment and sacrifice.

For me older women just tend to be more laid back in life like myself, and they've experienced different things and know what and what not to say and do to offend and hurt men" besides younger females are so career conscious and so far into fad happenings that they become oblivious to what it really take to please and bring happiness and total substance to a man.

...When I say older women I simply mean... A woman.

...Women who know that the trueness of life and relationships is love and caring every moment in everyday all the time in everyway, and I've seen countless younger women act and live more mature then some of the older ones.

Carl Nixon

Marriage material

After all the play, laughing and partying, one person and thing come to mind, material for marriage.

All along the way I've dated and seen females I would love to marry because of their outer beauty and attraction, but as the days go by I'm in the realization that these qualities alone don't warrant a marriage for me.

In life no one really know who they'll end up with, so I guess we go about life trying to take control of our own lives in the way in which we feel they should be lived, and a lot of times get involved with people we know aren't or won't be our best suits.

If I'm not feeling you from the start it don't matter what you say or do to have gotten me, my eye and ear is on the road ahead, always hoping someday I might find that someone that makes life worth living for me.

Too many people spend time in relationships for all the wrong reasons and afraid of getting out or don't know how or don't have the strength to get out when its no longer good for them.

…Material marriages are based on material things, but marriage materials I want to give my all with all my heart.

I didn't have to write this book, and who really cares anyway, but I wrote it because it's an expression of me, the things I've been hurt by, and the issues I had at heart.

I understand life is what you make it, but one can't over look the fact that we are all touched or affected in some way or another by what other's do, I tend to believe it's because deep down in our souls we have the need to be accepted and wanted by people' for we all make up the world.

I'd like to close by saying peace, love, and happiness be with all, and if there were even just a few things my opposite sex wanted to ever know about me'I hope she found it here.

Peace…

About the Author

Carl Encell Nixon was born in Detroit, Michigan in November 1969, but has lived in Indiana for eight years. He is single and his hobbies include basketball, writing, producing music, exercising, and watching movies. Male'in It is his first book.

www.ingramcontent.com/pod-product-compliance
Lightning Source LLC
Chambersburg PA
CBHW030356290526
45785CB00004B/1783